How do we know about Anglo-Saxon

by Patrick Wor

My title may raise eyebrows. Professional historians nowadays have a perceptible tendency to look gift horses in the mouth. Is it not enough that we do have historical as well as architectural evidence for Anglo-Saxon Deerhurst? Why should we worry about how we know? My answer to this question is best put in the words of James Campbell: 'our knowledge of so much hangs by so narrow a thread that it is certain as certain can be that there was a great deal about Anglo-Saxon England about which we do not know, and never will know, anything'. [1] I shall essentially be arguing in this lecture that we owe our historical evidence of pre-conquest Deerhurst to a series of lucky chances: a lawsuit involving a bishop who kept good archives; the murder by drunken Danes of an archbishop of Canterbury who had briefly been there; the link between its mid-eleventh century lord and a dominant influence on two important chronicles; and I shall conclude by suggesting that we are pretty lucky to have the church itself. Historians do not on the whole much like chance. It leaves them with little else to say. But it is appropriate that Anglo-Saxonists should sometimes dwell on it. The bulk of our knowledge of English history before 1066 derives directly or indirectly from a few towering figures: Bede, Alfred, Æthelwold, Wulfstan. Our ability to look beyond their dominant perspectives does indeed depend on a set of flukes: the preservation of Domesday Book above all; but also the obsession with monsters that induced an early-eleventh-century scribe to copy out *Beowulf*, a poem unparalleled not only in England but also in Europe as a whole; the ploughing away of part of the mound that caused tomb-robbers to miss the Sutton Hoo treasure by a few feet; the storm that persuaded the community of St. Cuthbert to abandon its projected journey to Ireland, whilst not preventing them from fishing the Lindisfarne Gospels out of a watery grave. As Anglo-Saxonists, we cultivate the borders of prehistory. We must never take knowledge for granted.

Another reasonable objection would be that we do *not* know much about pre-conquest Deerhurst. This is of course true. I shall here discuss one document preserved only in copies of two hundred or more years later; a few lines in a one saint's life written just after the conquest; and three entries in a pair of later-eleventh/early-twelfth-century chronicles – little enough to fill an hour. The fact remains that we know more about Anglo-Saxon Deerhurst than about nearly any other extant building with significant Anglo-Saxon elements. No two experts would supply quite the same *corpus* of Anglo-Saxon architecture, but a figure of some 250 churches with a plausible case for a pre-1066 construction would probably command consensus. [2] Discarding such obviously special cases as Hexham and Ripon, Monkwearmouth and Jarrow, Sherborne and one or more (?) Elmhams, a mere twenty-six feature in more or less acceptable narrative sources, usually no more than once; it is worth adding that five of the narrative references are from Bede and seven from the prolific Durham material. [3] Ten churches appear in documentary evidence (seven just once), and six of these are also found in narratives[4]. Well under half the Taylor-listed churches are mentioned in Domesday book – though since the great survey contrives to ignore Deerhurst too, its other oversights arouse no great surprise. The only profiles comparable with Deerhurst's are those of St. Mary's Stow, and the Kentish minsters, Dover, Minster-Sheppey and Reculver; we shall see that these are revealing parallels. Comparisons otherwise are with Repton (a couple of *Chronicle* entries, an early saint's *Life*, and a distant twelfth-century retrospect), Brixworth (one semi-documentary reference), or Wing (no evidence at all). It *is* evidently necessary to explain why Deerhurst should loom so relatively large; and if it is not necessary, it is still an opportunity to ponder what we know, or think we know.

Deerhurst makes its first appearance in the historical record in or shortly after 804. It is a fleeting appearance, but also an extremely important one. [5] The context is a document in which Æthelric son of Æthelmund announced that he had been vindicated before a synod of the archbishop of Canterbury, the king of the Mercians, and the leading ecclesiastical and secular officials of the kingdom, in his right to dispose as he wished of the estate at 'Westminster' (i.e. the minster of Westbury) which his 'kinsmen' had previously given to him. This right was vested in 'writings' that the archbishop perused before judging in Æthelric's favour. The implication is that these writings were the 'books' (i.e. charters) whereby the estate was originally granted to his kin. The text goes on to tell how, on returning from a pilgrimage to Rome, he declared before another synod what he intended to do with his 'hereditas'. The central issue was once again what was to happen to Westbury: Æthelric assigned it (with 'Stoke') to his mother, Ceolburh, with reversion after her death to the church of Worcester. The intention was evidently that Worcester's long-term interest in the estate would encourage it to protect Ceolburh 'against the claims of the Berkeley people' (as Æthelric called them): he envisaged that she might well have to make out a legal case against them and would presumably need allies. But Westbury was not the only property at stake. Æthelric also bequeathed a thirty hide estate to Gloucester and another eleven hides to one Wærferth, also with reversion to Worcester. Most important for our purposes, he granted four estates to 'the place which is called Deerhurst for me and for my father Æthelmund, if it should happen that *my* body rests there'. I emphasize the word 'my' because the sense of his proviso must surely be that his father's body already was buried at Deerhurst.

How are these transactions to be explained? The first point to make is that Æthelric was right to be worried about 'Berkeley people'. Twenty years after the synod that had originally found for him, Bishop Heahberht of Worcester appeared before a similar council in dispute 'with the *familia* at Berkeley about the *hereditas* of Æthelric son of Æthelmund, that is the monastery called Westbury'.[6] He still had the 'books' as well as the property, and was therefore allowed to organize an oath of 'servants of God, priests, deacons and many monks' that Westbury was indeed his. The oath duly took place, and the document recording these proceedings gives the names of no less than fifty-six of those who took it, three abbots, six deacons and the rest priests; the bishop had evidently rustled up a fair proportion of his diocesan manpower in his own support. The prolonged bitterness of the disputes over 'the inheritance of Æthelric' is probably the very reason why so much of the documentation about it survives. Indeed, I have argued elsewhere that Worcester almost certainly extended it by resorting to the forgery of charters whereby Westbury was granted directly to them rather than to Æthelmund, while a connected property at Stoke went not to Æthelmund with full freedom of disposition, but to Æthelmund with reversion to Worcester after two lives.[7]

If we are to understand how cases like this arose and persisted, we have to appreciate that it is not a simple matter of ecclesiastical principle at war with worldly interests (though church records are of course prone to make it sound like that). To begin with the case for Æthelric's and the bishop's opponents, we must look, for a brief if doubtless painful moment, into the question of 'bookland', one of the real hornets' nests of Anglo Saxon studies.[8] Books, that is charters, were the principal means of bestowing land on the Church. Since they were meant for the Church, they had to be *permanent* gifts, gifts in perpetuity; whereas there is evidence that gifts made by kings or lords to lay followers were not normally permanent but revocable, on the death or dissatisfaction of either party. On the other hand, the permanently held property of early Anglo-Saxon laymen was normally subject to the claims of their kin. It was also necessary, therefore, that land that was intended for transmission to the Church should be *freely disposable* by its recipient. Thus, the two points stressed by the earliest charters are that donors are granting for ever and irrevocably, and that donees may do what they like with what they have devoutly received. But there is a critical catch. What do owners normally like to do with their property? The answer, surely, is to give it to the *heir of their choice.* This may be an elder son already well-provided for , a younger son or daughter that is otherwise missing out, a favourite maiden-aunt, or a cat's home. What owners do not like is being told what to do with it. In an early medieval context, those demanding that property be disposed of in a particular way were the kin, the family entitled to retain hereditary lands according to traditional custom. The equivalent to the cat's home was the Church, though its chances were perhaps rather better in that one's best hope of eternal salvation was burial among grateful priests who would pray for that eternally. But there was a very real risk that this new type of perpetually tenured gift would be transferred to *chosen* members of a family. Perhaps the likeliest outcome was that churches would be founded for the immediate benefit of a family's disadvantaged members, most obviously an unmarriageable female, who would then safeguard the long-term interests of the wider kin by the prayers she organized.[9] If this were what happened, then there is a further twist. The more bookland was *de facto* confined to a family over several generations, the more like family property it would come to seem, and thus the more likely to be effectively claimed as inherited property by the kin.

This, at all events, is exactly what did happen. We see it in a furious letter that the Venerable Bede wrote in the last year of his life, denouncing the proliferation of 'monasteries only in name': 'laymen under the pretext of founding monasteries buy lands on which they may more freely devote themselves to lust, and in addition cause them to be ascribed to them in hereditary right by royal edicts'; 'the very same men now are occupied with wives and the procreation of children, now rising from their beds perform with assiduous attention what should be done within the precincts of monasteries (a very ugly and unheard-of spectacle)'.[10] Bede's language is of course highly coloured, but it is significant that he already describes grants by 'royal edicts' (charters) as 'hereditary right'. A more dispassionate impression of the same process comes from eighth- and ninth-century charters which record the descent of churches within families, or even stipulate that this should be so.[11] Late in Alfred's reign, a nobleman successfully sued a member of the church of Worcester for possession of land that a charter of his relative, King Coenwulf, had ordered to be restricted to his kin; and Alfred himself issued a law allowing kins to make such dispositions.[12] Words meaning 'inheritance' were by now habitually used as the Westbury documents use them: for property obtained by book, hence *not* in theory heritable by customary norms.[13] In short, what had originally been meant to create church property which was *free* from the claims of kindred came increasingly to mean property in which the kin had a legitimate interest.

The complexities of this subject readily explain why historians have disputed it so bitterly. They also explain why there were a whole number of later-eighth and ninth-century disputes over the disposition of bookland, and why Æthelric's inheritance gave rise to one of them. Deerhurst itself was presumably the family monastery *par excellence*, if Æthelmund was buried there, and Æthelric expected to be. It does correspondingly well under the terms of his will. Westbury was a lavishly endowed minster which Æthelric might have hoped to keep in his family, but which it was prudent to promise to Worcester in return for its protection of his mother's short-term tenure. Ceolburh herself died in 807 as an abbess, of Berkeley itself according to a later Worcester source.[14] Berkeley may therefore have been *her* family monastery, and have expected to lay hands on Westbury because Æthelric or Æthelmund had already put her in possession of it: they could not — or would not — distinguish between '*hereditas*' that was actually vested in a charter, so freely disposable, and genuinely inherited family property that was subject to their claims. Putting it another way, Æthelric claimed freedom of disposition, and proceeded to use it in his mother's interest. It is hardly surprising that the 'Berkeley people' were confused.[15]

It is an unedifying as well as complex story. But there is, as I say, more to it than a conflict between worldliness and reform. The bishop's case was nothing like so 'open-and-shut' as it seems to our principled eyes. At much the same time as Æthelric's family was establishing its ecclesiastical empire, papal charters were allowing Mercian kings to exercise patronage over their family monasteries. When Bishop Heahberht's great contemporary, Archbishop Wulfred, challenged King Coenwulf about the abbeys ruled by his daughter, he may have found the pope against him, and his victory was both long-delayed and Pyrrhic.[16] Even the formidable Carolingian episcopate was humiliated when it tried to put reforming principles into practice. My tentative suggestion in the present context is that the bishop of Worcester had to pay for his eventual success at Westbury by giving up hope of doing anything about Deerhurst itself, the house where Æthelmund lay buried and which, if it was indeed the principal family monastery, must have mattered most to Æthelric. Kindred claims had deep roots in the psychology of the early medieval western nobility. It would take several centuries of reform to pull them up. A last point is one I have made before, but it will bear repetition in this of all settings. Historians who bemoan the decline of Bede's church into worldly values need to appreciate that it is inseparable from much of what they admire. What we look at in this church comes from the wealth and love of lavish display of a powerful local family; that is to say, we owe it to two of the values of an aristocracy, for whom the integrity of family property was a third. The world of fallen humanity is not so full of rich young men like Bede's Benedict Bishop, ready to give away their wealth so as to receive a hundredfold from Christ, that we can reasonably expect to have the artistic patronage without the rest of the value system that made it possible.

So the first thing I wish to register is that we owe our earliest and crucial glimpse of Deerhurst to a prolonged wrangle between the family of the lay patrons responsible for the splendour we see around us and the reforming (if itself not entirely disinterested) zeal of bishops determined to rein in such claims. Specifically, we owe it to the excellence of the archives kept at Worcester from the late-seventh century, and carefully transcribed in what is by far the earliest English cartulary. The only remote parallel is Canterbury cathedral itself, which managed to pass on a large number of documents in their original form, though only from 798.[17] This is no doubt why Kentish churches are the only ones that feature as prominently as Deerhurst in the documentary records. It is pertinent to note that at least one of these gave rise to the same conflict of Church authorities and secular patrons as Westbury, and at the same time.[18] There must have been many more such churches, and may have been many more such conflicts.

We may now pass on to Deerhurst's equally brief appearance in tenth-century history. Osbern, precentor of Canterbury, wrote a *Life of St. Ælfheah,* the archbishop who was killed in 1012 by Danes who had just looted a wine-ship, after he had refused to burden his flock any further with their demands for tribute (he would presumably have taken a rueful view of Kipling's much-quoted observation that 'once you have paid the Danegeld/you will never get rid of the Dane').[19] Osbern says that Ælfheah began his monastic experience in a 'monastery called Deerhurst; and, inasmuch as the place was sparsely inhabited, virtue made those who did live there most admirable'. What follows is an equally over-written and imprecise account of how Ælfheah cultivated the monastic virtues; until he 'seized the path of a stricter life, and entered single combat with the malign enemy' as a hermit at Bath, where he soon gathered a following and established a monastery. This story raises more problems than orthodox historiography is ready to admit. Nothing is said of Dunstan (otherwise Osbern's special hero), who is usually credited with the re-establishment of Bath.[20] Nor is any mention made of Oswald, who is customarily found at the top of the monastic 'family tree' in which Deerhurst stands. There is in fact no evidence that Oswald had anything at all to do with Deerhurst; Dom David Knowles's only reason for including it among his refoundations was that he could thus make up the total of seven claimed by Oswald's biographer, Byrhtferth.[21] But seven is a suspiciously mystical number, and Byrhtferth was much given to such casts of mind.[22] If there is no reason to think that Deerhurst was ever part of Oswald's connection, then there is no reason either to include it among the targets of the notorious Ealdorman Ælfhere's 'anti-monastic reaction.'[23]

We need not disbelieve Osbern's story entirely. It is supported by William of Malmesbury and by the *Chronicle* of John of Worcester (which, hard as they try, historians seem to be unable to get out of the habit of attributing to 'Florence').[24] But it is still the case that Osbern's account of Ælfheah at Deerhurst leaves almost no cliché of monastic hagiography undeployed. He was writing his *Life* to answer the vigorously expressed doubts of Archbishop Lanfranc about his predecessor's claim to martyrdom (Lanfranc was no doubt sensitive about those who achieved martyrdom by resisting foreign invaders).[25] The signs are that he knew no more of Ælfheah's earlier life than a pair of place-names. There seem to be two possibilities. The Deerhurst joined by Ælfheah could have been a community of dedicated reformers who had established themselves independently of any great patron, as regularly happened on the continent (where scholars have now learned to be chary of 'family-trees').[26] It may then have simply subsided into comfortable 'normalcy' after the first enthusiastic generation, with no need for anti-monastic reactions. Alternatively, it might not in fact have been a reformed community at all, but the sort of secular college that it had presumably been since the ninth-century and would again be in the eleventh. Ælfheah would then have been individually called to reform from a conventional background; and if Deerhurst were never reformed, it need never have been attacked. In any event, Ælfheah's residence at Deerhurst seems secure. So it is that a post-conquest controversy about an individual's status as a martyr provides our one link between the ninth century and the eleventh.

It remains to consider the entries relating to Deerhurst in the later part of the *Anglo-Saxon Chronicle*, and in the closely related *Chronicle* of John of Worcester. These entries are just three: first, for the year 1016, the text of the *Anglo-Saxon Chronicle* known as 'D', which was written in the latter decades of the eleventh-century and breaks off in 1079, informs us that Olney, site of the treaty between Cnut and Edmund Ironside that concluded the hostilities of that gruelling year, was 'near Deerhurst': while John says that the two kings first met at Deerhurst, Edmund on the west bank of the Severn and Cnut on the east, before proceeding to negotiations at Olney, an island in the river itself. The second is for the year 1053: again, it is the 'D' manuscript of the *Anglo-Saxon Chronicle* which records the death at Deerhurst of Ælfric, brother of Odda, followed by his burial at Pershore; and this time John of Worcester merely supplies a calendar date for his death. Finally, the 'C' as well as the 'D' *Chronicle* versions enter the death on 31st August 1056 of Earl Odda (evidently the afore-mentioned brother of Ælfric), both saying that he became a monk before he died and that he too was buried at Pershore; but 'D' alone adds a tribute to his pure and noble character; and John records that he died at Deerhurst, and that Bishop Ealdred of Worcester had admitted him to monastic status.[27] This is admittedly not much. But it is more, I repeat, than we have for all but a very select few of the pre-conquest churches whose fabric still substantially survives. Of particular interest is that some of it reads very like local colour. So *can* it be said that these entries exist because they were, in some sense, of local concern?

This question, unfortunately, launches us onto the quagmire of *Anglo-Saxon Chronicle* scholarship. Although the *Chronicle* is axiomatically the most important source for English history from 731 to the twelfth century (E.A. Freeman, the erratic Victorian polymath, thought that it belonged on all true-born Englishmen's bedside tables, along with the Bible and Shakespeare), it is astonishingly difficult to find any consensus on where or when any one part of any one text was written, or on how the relationship of the different versions may be explained. In any *Chronicle* study of less than monograph length, argument has to make way for hypothesis, where W's deduction is X's hunch, and Y's rigour is Z's abuse of Occam's razor. Yet *Chronicle* forays can have *something* of the charm of an explorer's tale. And the expedition I wish to launch here may cast further light on a figure who was of considerable importance in the history of mid-eleventh-century England generally and of Deerhurst specifically. In embarking on it, I shall move with all due deliberation, sticking to what little common ground there is, though with a wary eye for its erosion by modern research.[28]

The temptation to speak of the *Anglo-Saxon Chronicle* in the singular is like Original Sin: irresistible, redeemable, but for all that quite wrong. There was, to be sure, a core text common to all versions, which was evidently put together in 891/2 at or in the neighbourhood of King Alfred's court. But, as they stand, the seven and a bit *Chronicle* manuscripts should be regarded as so many distinct *Chronicles* . The next point to appreciate is that three of these, the versions known as 'E' and 'F' as well as 'D' itself, are conflations of two or more earlier versions, put together after 1066 when there was a premium on the recovery of a vanishing Anglo-Saxon past. The Latin *Chronicle* of John of Worcester is another text of this type. Since these chronicles represent editorial efforts, they also reflect an element of editorial choice, which makes it difficult to draw any very clear conclusions about the identity or localization of their authors. It is misleading to argue from entries relating to particular places or areas, because these could have been selected from *one* of that chronicle's *sources*. It is even less justifiable to exclude a possible provenance on the basis that a text omits items that we would then expect to find; they may have been editorially omitted for reasons that we are in no position to know. We have to look not at the details but at the overall shape of a *Chronicle* text, to study the macrocosmic rather than the microcosmic patterns.

A first point at least is quite clear. John of Worcester's *Chronicle* was certainly written at Worcester in the 1120s and 1130s. The characteristic hand of what is evidently an autograph manuscript occurs throughout a number of books of definite or probable Worcester origin. To that extent, my main question is already answered. If 'D' did not survive, John would still supply us with all we know about eleventh-century Deerhurst. But this would still leave us with the question of his sources. Because we do have the 'D' *Chronicle*, we can say that one of them was either 'D' itself, or something very like it. It is on 'D', therefore, that the argument needs to focus.[29] The *prima facie* conclusion from its closeness to John is that 'D' too is from Worcester: the 'Worcester Chronicle' is what Freeman unhesitatingly called it. An important point in Worcester's favour is that it was certainly there in the sixteenth century, when Archbishop Parker's indefatigable secretary, John Joscelyn, also called it the 'Worcester Chronicle', and said that it was still in the church library. The case for Worcester was powerfully restated in 1940 by Sir Ivor Atkins in a paper which, as we shall see, came closer than anyone yet has to solving the problem.[30]

But the case for Worcester is not in fact secure. In the first place, it is not a conclusive argument that 'D' was there in the sixteenth century, or even in the twelfth. One of the things that is increasingly clear about twelfth-century Worcester is the special effort that it put into the reconstruction of the Anglo-Saxon past. One of its fruits was precisely John of Worcester's *Chronicle*. Such was its reputation for historical expertise that Eadmer, the Canterbury historian and biographer of

Anselm, twice consulted Prior Nicholas of Worcester about historical issues. One of these was the rights of the metropolitan see of York in Scotland – about which one might have expected Eadmer to know enough already. But Nicholas was almost certainly the Englishman, Æthelred, who had been a special protegé of the sainted Bishop Wulfstan, and who therefore had links with the Old English past unmatched by any other leading churchmen of the early twelfth century.[31] It is thus not at all unlikely that the 'D' *Chronicle* was among the materials assembled by Worcester's early-twelfth-century specialists, but had not itself been written there. A second point that weighs very heavily against a Worcester origin for 'D', despite my warning of the pitfalls of arguments from omission, is that (unlike John) it says nothing about that see's great hero of the later-eleventh century, St. Wulfstan.

This point had already been registered by the *Anglo-Saxon Chronicle's* first real editor, Charles Plummer, who himself proposed nearby Evesham instead.[32] Atkins dealt conclusively with the Evesham hypothesis, but failed to account satisfactorily for Wulfstan's absence. This strategic error exposed the whole flank of his argument to the uniquely heavy artillery of Professor Dorothy Whitelock – or, more precisely, to the batteries of Sir Frank Stenton which she fired (as was her wont) on his behalf. What Stenton and Whitelock spotted about the 'D' *Chronicle* was its special interest in the affairs of the sainted Queen Margaret of Scotland, herself an English princess.[33] 'D', together with 'E', form what is called 'the Northern Recension' of the *Chronicle*. Three of its features are particularly important: it inserts into the core pre-892 text a number of items of northern interest, derived from Bede and from a set of eighth-century annals that very probably originated at York (they refer to York as '*ceaster*, the city' without further specification); it includes an annal for 959 in the ubiquitous idiom of Archbishop Wulfstan of York (1002-23); and its 1065-79 annals (before 'D' breaks off) resume a distinctly northern orientation. 'D' has a more pronounced interest in Scotland than 'E', has a further Wulfstanian passage at 975 (though making no reference, unlike 'E', to Wulfstan's death), and gives more details about northern affairs 926-58, 1026-55, and again from 1065. The Stenton/

Whitelock proposal is therefore that 'D' was a *Chronicle* made in the North, quite possibly for the Anglo-Scottish royal court.

Anglo-Saxon historians differ from Professor Whitelock at their peril, even when her guns have sadly fallen silent. But the 'northern case' as she deploys it is nonetheless vulnerable in its turn. The first objection (of which she was well aware) is that the Deerhurst entries are one of a series of what might be called 'Mercian' or 'West Midland' items in 'D's' otherwise 'northern' sections: identification of Pucklechurch as the place where King Edmund was stabbed to death; a Worcester/Droitwich earthquake sensed as far away as Derby; display of the Welsh prince Rhys's head at Gloucester 'on the eve of Epiphany'.[34] Second, it has now been shown that Northumbrian annals in Latin which are related to the 'northern recension's' eighth-century additions were written in their extant form by Byrhtferth, the Ramsey monk who, as biographer of Oswald and Ecgwine, obviously had close West Midland contacts.[35] Access to 'northern' sources was therefore possible in a 'southern' context. The fact that the 'northern recension' of the Chronicle can call York simply *the* city' means merely than that its source passed through a 'York phase', as is anyway intrinsically likely. Third and above all (and as Whitelock again stressed herself) it is a critical clue to the solution of this whole mystery that the sees of York and Worcester were combined for fifty years from Oswald's accession in 971 until Archbishop Wulfstan's death, again in 1040-1, and finally under Archbishop Ealdred in 1061-2 until an increasingly reform-minded papacy indignantly terminated this means of allaying official anxiety about the questionable loyalty and unquestionable poverty of the northern archbishopric. It follows that passages in Wulfstanian style are just as likely to have been included at Worcester as at York. It follows too that we can explain both the 'Worcester' features that underpinned Atkins' case and those that directed the Stenton/Whitelock gaze northward, without discarding the strengths of either hypothesis. Best of all, it allows a first sight of the goal of this tortuous progress: Bishop Ealdred of Worcester, future archbishop of York, who on 12th April 1056 dedicated Odda's chapel at Deerhurst; and later that summer, also at Deerhurst, bestowed monastic orders on the dying earl.

Odda's Chapel, Deerhurst, dedicated by Bishop Ealdred in 1056. The chapel now adjoins Abbot's Court farmhouse.

I have said that *Chronicle* analysis may have more to learn from macrocosmic patterns than microcosmic details. Ealdred's prominence in the 'D' text is so macrocosmic that not much about it is not thereby explained. Take a very simple indicator first. One of the glories of Plummer's *Chronicle* edition is its 145-page index. On what is admittedly no more than an 'instant scan', Ealdred is found to occupy thirty-three lines of it, with twenty-six listed entries of which over half are in 'D' alone. This is more than any other non-royal individual bar three: Earl Godwine, who was the father of a future king, and whose prominence is swollen by the uniquely detailed records of the crisis surrounding his exile and return in 1051-2; Archbishop Dunstan, who has only fourteen entries, and whose forty-five lines owe more to Plummer's notes than to *Chronicle* texts; and Archbishop Lanfranc, the great bulk of whose entries derive from the Latin 'Acts of Lanfranc' added to a single manuscript at Canterbury. So mere statistics make a strong case for Ealdred, and especially in relation to the 'D' text.

Then, quite a number of 'D's' special features make sense in terms of what Ealdred is known or likely to have done or thought. The obvious ones are its records, not in 'C' or 'E', of Ealdred's succession to the see of Worcester in 1046, his assumption of responsibility for the abbey of Winchcombe in 1053, the fact that, as diocesan, he nonetheless permitted the bishop of Lichfield to consecrate the church of Evesham in 1054 (when, as we shall see in a moment, he was on other business), his own consecration of Gloucester Abbey and pilgrimage to Jerusalem in 1058 (making 'a worthy gift for our Lord's tomb of a golden chalice worth five marks, of very wonderful workmanship'), and his receipt of the archiepiscopal *pallium* from the Pope (without mention of his rebuff for pluralism) in 1061.[36] Another well-known characteristic of 'D' is its neutrality in the political struggles of the house of Godwine with its many enemies. It is thus interesting that 'D' should once more be alone in saying that Ealdred was instructed by the king to intercept Harold and his brother as they took flight in 1051, but 'could not - or would not'.[37] We can also note the special emphasis laid by 'D' on the promises of good government that Ealdred received from William the Conqueror before he crowned him on Christmas Day 1066. A story still treasured in York tradition centuries later told how Ealdred obliged the king to punish an oppressive sheriff by robustly reminding him of his promises.[38] But perhaps the clinching consideration, and certainly the most interesting in its implications for the fraught politics of the period, is the very preoccupation of 'D' with Queen Margaret and her family that pointed Stenton and Whitelock towards the Scottish court. As 'D' alone tells us, Ealdred spent nearly a year in 1054-5 at Cologne 'on the king's business', and there is little doubt that the business in question was the recall of Edward 'the Exile', son of the Confessor's half-brother and Margaret's father. 'D' is again on its own in dwelling at length on Edward's return, origin and almost immediate lamentable death in 1057. Finally, and most suggestively, it is 'D' that says that Archbishop Ealdred and the citizens of London wanted to make Margaret's brother,

Edgar Ætheling, king after Hastings 'as was his due'.[39] It is thus entirely to be expected that any associate of Ealdred's should retain the sort of interest in this family's Scottish experiences that is 'D's' hallmark.

An Ealdred hypothesis permits most of 'D's' problems to fall into place. A source associated with him would of course be interested both in York and Worcester down to 1062, but would from then abandon any concern with Worcester and its saintly bishop for the more radically northern bias that persisted after his death in 1069. Quite apart from his transfer to York, he and his Norman successor had a number of legal run-ins with St. Wulfstan. If a certain coolness about him could be found anywhere in England, it would perhaps be at York.[40] Had Atkins given this solution more than a passing glance in a paper that otherwise said nearly all that I have, he would not have drawn Whitelock's fire, and might be considered to have solved the problem. His only substantial objection (other than 'D's' later Worcester provenance) was that the text makes a mistake in 1072 which should have been inconceivable for a member of the York clergy. But Ealdred was the patron and reformer of several northern churches, in any one of which a careless scribe could have misconstrued the text before him. And since it was from the West Midlands (particularly Evesham) that the North was re-colonized for the monastic life in the decades after 1070, maintenance of the sort of contacts that would have enabled Worcester's specialists to set hands on 'D' in the first half of the twelfth century is not at all implausible.[41] So long as York itself is excluded, the case that 'D' was compiled in the North, and very largely from sources associated closely with Ealdred, appears to stand as steadily as any hypothesis can on such quaking terrain.[42]

This painstaking ramble through far from promising scenery is thus of interest to more than *Anglo-Saxon Chronicle* afficionadoes. If the argument holds, the 'D' *Chronicle* is itself evidence of the political, administrative and ecclesiastical horizons of one of the key personalities in later Old English history, one who, as much as any other (and even if not for long), represented a bridge across the chasm of 1066. Among these horizons was Deerhurst. We need look no further for the reason why Deerhurst alone, of the Worcester diocese's many minsters, should appear in the chronicles. It was important to those of Ealdred's entourage who followed him to York (whence 'D') or stayed at Worcester (whence John), because Ealdred and Odda were close. In this connection, I have a final suggestion that returns us neatly to where we were before. It will be recalled that Archbishop Wulfstan's death in 1023 is unexpectedly overlooked by 'D'. I did not then say what replaces it: an elaborate account of the translation of the martyred Archbishop Ælfheah. If Ælfheah's memory was in any way preserved at Deerhurst, as is not in the least unlikely, then it also makes sense that his interment as one of the English church's greatest heroes should have seemed important in Ealdred's circle.[43] This in turn may be the reason why John chose to record Ælfheah's Deerhurst episode in his own *Chronicle*.

I have been arguing so far as if the existence of two magnificent Anglo-Saxon buildings at Deerhurst were what can be taken for granted, and the availability of any *historical* information about them were what needs explaining. I shall finish by reversing the argument. One reason, as is now generally agreed, why so much Anglo-Saxon building seems relatively unimpressive is that all the wealthier and more important buildings were comprehensively rebuilt when improved later medieval architectural technology made this possible. Those left more or less as they stood were the poorer and less important. Now, there are in fact many reasons for thinking that Deerhurst was anything but unimportant. Æthelmund was the man who ran the sub-kingdom of the Hwicce for King Offa after its 'native' dynasty disappeared. Odda was probably a kinsman of King Edward, was certainly one of his most prominent nobles and may possibly have himself held administrative responsibility for the West Midlands.[44] No church so favoured by such figures can have failed to matter. Nor was it impoverished. Deerhurst's Domesday assessment of 119 hides valued at £67 10/- is hugely greater than that of manors associated with almost any other pre-conquest church whose fabric still substantially survives above ground. If it had retained this value, it would have eclipsed Sherborne cathedral or Burton Abbey and ranked not far below Worcester itself.[45] So, instead of asking why Deerhurst gets fleetingly into the historical record, I ought probably to have asked why, alone among churches of comparable significance and wealth, it is still extant as a largely Anglo-Saxon building.

This introduces the last of the sources for Anglo-Saxon Deerhurst; and it nicely makes the point about precarious information, because it is lost. Edward the Confessor's writ granting half of Deerhurst to his cherished abbey of Westminster is extant, as is an associated boundary clause and a number of fraudulent texts confirming the bequest. But the writ that gave the other half *via* his personal doctor, Baldwin, to Baldwin's home abbey of Saint-Denis is known only from William the Conqueror's confirmation of 1069.[46] Now, the diversion of the estate must obviously have affected Deerhurst's fortunes, especially as Westminster got the more valuable part while Saint-Denis was lumbered with the church itself. All the same, Saint-Denis' manor was still worth £26 10/-. That Deerhurst was not rebuilt may be as much because of a lack of interest as a lack of funds. The abbots of Saint-Denis were among the most influential builders of the Middle Ages. Abbot Suger was pioneer and propagandist of the Gothic style.[47] But it was his own church that concerned him, not those of its overseas dependants. So long as the revenues flowed (and so long, no doubt, as the church still stood up) Deerhurst could be left as it was. Had it come into the hands of a great lay patron, it would surely have been magnificently rebuilt, as Robert Fitz Haimo rebuilt no less wealthy Tewkesbury nearby. In other words, the survival of what William of Malmesbury, in a characteristically graphic phrase, called 'this empty image of antiquity', to house a special lecture series may be the consequence of an absentee landlord's benign neglect.[48]

What I have been saying in this lecture could thus be summarized in the proposition that Deerhurst was important to important people in Anglo-Saxon times, but it was not of *front-rank* importance. That is precisely its value to a historian. Returning to what I said at the outset, our view of Anglo-Saxon history is dictated by a very few supremely articulate people. We are in danger of missing the rich variety of early English culture if our impressions of what happened and what mattered are merely those of the dominant sources. Bede's dens of vice were the minsters which were what most people saw of the Church in action for centuries. More was happening in the tenth-century Church than the Tenth-Century Reformation. Not everybody in the reign of Edward the Confessor was supporting the succession of one or other of the protagonists at Hastings. To lecture at Jarrow is to encounter an idealist's vision of history. To lecture at Deerhurst is to remember that there is more to history than ideals.

APPENDIX:Westbury and Stoke

My paper of 1986 (n. 5 below) argued the probability that two of the charters on which Worcester based its rights to the inheritance of Æthelric were forged or doctored in its interest, and that this was done by the church of Worcester in order to promote its suit at the synod of 824. My argument has been questioned (though not repudiated) by Patrick Sims-Williams, *Religion and Literature in Western England, 600-800* (Cambridge, 1990), pp. 155 (n.61), 176. The possibility that the bishop of Worcester had to resort to (doubtless pious) fraud in order to sustain a case against the family solidarities of lay patrons is germane to an understanding of why and how churches like Deerhurst came to exist. I therefore take this opportunity to give my reasons for still thinking that he did.

The charters in question are S 59, which appears to survive in an original form, and S 146, which is preserved in the early-eleventh-century Worcester cartulary attributed to Hemming and also in another eleventh-century Worcester cartulary. S 59, dated 770, presents an adapted version of S 58, dated 767, in that five hides at Stoke Priors (Aston) which had been given to Æthelmund outright were now to be possessed only in his lifetime and for that of two heirs, after which 'the land with the deeds is to be given back (*reddatur*) to the church of Worcester'. On the other hand, S 146 is an alternative version of S 139, in that the latter granted a fifty-five hide estate at Westbury to Æthelmund, while the former gave sixty hides to Worcester (neither is dated, but both have the same dating range, 793-6).

It must be granted that the circumstances are indeed *prima facie* suspicious. Dr Sims-Williams, following a line of thought already advanced by Professor A. Bruckner, *Chartae Latinae Antiquiores* IV (Olten & Lausanne, 1967) no. 274, thinks it 'not impossible that S 59 is a revised copy, not necessarily forged, issued late in Offa's reign with the added consent of his heirs (as seen on the dorse), of a lost charter of 770'; and rather less tentatively that the Stoke referred to by Æthelric in his dispositions of 804 was Stoke Bishop, adjoining Westbury itself, in which case Stoke Priors would not be in dispute, and there would be no call for a doctored charter. These issues can to taken in reverse order.

1) There is no doubt that the Worcester cartularists came to identify the Stoke of Æthelric's document (S 1187) with Stoke Bishop. Part I of Hemming's cartulary (ed. T. Hearne, *Hemingi Chartularium Ecclesiae Wigorniensis*, Oxford, 1723, pp. 101-6) sandwiches Æthelric's statement between S146, Worcester's Westbury grant, and the charter of 883 that granted it Stoke Bishop (S 218), and supplies a linking rubic '*Carta Æthelrici de Westburh 7 Stoc'*. A list in the other eleventh-century cartulary seems to regard Westbury and Stoke as a single unit. But this cartulary is often slapdash, and even Hemming Part I may simply have been misled by the proximity of Westbury and Stoke Bishop into falsely identifying the Stoke to which Æthelric refers. Dr Sims-Williams notes that the forty-three hides allocated to Westbury in the version of Æthelric's will given by Hemming Part II combines with the twelve hides of Stoke Bishop to make up

the fifty-five at which Westbury was assessed in S 139. But it seems clear that forty-three is the hidage of *Westbury and Stoke together*: '*terram xliii manentium æt Westmynster et ad Stoce*' (Heming, *Chartularium*, p. 448) corresponds precisely to '*terram illam æt Westmynster 7 æt Stoce*' in Part I (*ibid.*, p. 472), which Dr Sims-Williams takes to denote their unity. There is in fact no other basis for thinking that Westbury was ever assessed at forty-three hides: it has fifty in Domesday. The Hemming Part II figure sems likely to derive from a muddled cartularist's *subtraction* of Stoke Bishop's twelve hides from the fifty-five of S 139. Besides, the words '*terram illam æt Westmynster 7 æt Stoce*' need no more indicate *contiguous* areas than '*xi manentium Bremesgrefan 7 Feccanhom*' (i.e. Bromsgrove and Feckenham) earlier in the text. If they did betoken a unit, this could have been a 'discrete' estate of Westbury and Stoke *Priors* (five hides); that would explain how the fifty-five hides of S 139 became sixty in S 146, which would in turn explain why no Stoke is mentioned in S 1433 (824). Other points are that S 218 (883), in transferring Stoke Bishop from Berkeley to Worcester, gives no hint that it had once been disputed between them, or indeed that Worcester had any prior claim on it at all; and that even if Westbury and Stoke (Bishop) *had* formed an ancient unit (as argued, on the basis of a somewhat indiscrimate use of charter and Domesday evidence, by C.S. Taylor in a paper on 'The Pre-Domesday Hide of Gloucestershire', *Trans. Bristol & Gloucs Arch. Soc.* XVIII (1893-4), pp. 288-319, to which Dr Sims-William refers) it by no means follows that it had all been granted to Æthelmund, or was all at his son's disposal in 804.

2) Even if Stoke in S 1187 *were* Stoke Bishop, the evident sensitivity of the 'inheritance of Æthelric' might still have prompted Worcester to adjust Æthelmund's Stoke Priors charter. S 59 remains suspect in itself on two grounds. First, the witnessing of the 'heirs' on its dorse can certainly not have coincided with that of the others on its face: Queen Cynethryth and Prince Ecgfrith do not otherwise witness reliable charters until 779 (S 114) and 785 (S 123) respectively, and Princess Ælfflæd recurs only in S 127 (787), whereas Eata and Eadbald do not appear in acceptable texts after 775 (SS 63, 1411). Unless the attestations of the royal family are in a different ink (as cannot be proved under present conditions, and is not claimed by any authority), S59 must be either an accurate copy of a conflated text or a bogus conflation of lists from the 760s and 780s. Confirmation by queen and children alone is otherwise unparalleled, so the latter possibility seems likelier. Second, there is '*reddatur*'. Terminology should perhaps not be pressed too far. But elsewhere the word is used in leases or with a general sense of exchange or reversion: (following chronological order and ignoring spuriously early or otherwise irrelevant texts) S 1254, 109, 1255, 62, 1430, 149, 155, 1258, 1613, 1431, 1264, 1262, 1434, 1436, 1414, 281, 192, as well as S 1187, 1433; of service due etc. in BCS 310, S 180, 186, 1414; and on innumerable occasions of account rendered (or reward received) at Judgement Day. It seems to mean no more than 'hand over' (as in a hypothetically authentic S 59) in S 1429, 108(?), 1257(?), 185, 1436(?), 1414; but there is often a sense of reversion even here, and a noteworthy proportion of these texts are dispute records. It seems to have been a word that occurred to earlier charter draftsmen when thinking of what was *due* to them. But why should what had been given to

Æthelmund have become 'due' to Worcester? As for the change of date from S 58's 767 to S 59's 770: the Worcester community *knew* from S 1187 that Æthelric had deposited copies of his dispositions with his 'friends'. They faced the risk that these would have extended to a copy of S 58. Hence, they *had* to produce a version of the text whose import was that the 767 arrangements had been superseded shortly afterwards.

S 146 is another matter. In 1986, I thought that it may not have been forged before the eleventh century; but there is reason to think that it too was a product of the early-ninth-century crisis. Its witness-list is right for late in Offa's reign, but with the crucial reservation that Archbishop Hygeberht, Offa's controversial new metropolitan of Lichfield, is missing, though the other archibishop and two other Mercian bishops are present. It may not be coincidence that the only other case of his absence since 781, even in his mere episcopal days, is S 132, a Canterbury forgery (cf. Brooks, *Canterbury* (as n. 16 below), pp. 119, 350 (n. 36). To omit Hygeberht need not have occured to a forger of the eleventh century, when the whole saga must have been long forgotten everywhere except Canterbury. But in the fraught circumstances of the 820s, it might very well strike a wise Worcester scribe that Hygeberht's presence would risk the support of a still sensitive Canterbury. If, however, S 146 is a forgery of the same date as S 59, why is it so different? A not unreasonable guess is that Worcester did not then have the text of S 139, as they already did that of S 58, and so had no opportunity to adjust the disposition of an extant charter. They therefore had to create a rival text on the basis of some other exemplar, and hope that their credit outweighed their opponents'.

Professor Brooks has conclusively shown that Archbishop Wulfred did employ forgery in pursuit of a case over the Kentish minsters that precisely coincided with the Westbury dispute (below, n. 16). There is not enough evidence of the right type to make as strong a case that Worcester forged its Westbury and Stoke deeds. Yet if this is what Canterbury did, it is at least not inconceivable, and is perhaps not unlikely, that Worcester pursued the same objective by the same means.

NOTES

1.   J. Campbell, ed., *The Anglo-Saxons* (2nd edn, London, 1991), p. 246. I wish to thank Mr Arnold Porter and the Friends of Deerhurst Church for the invitation to collect and publish these miscellaneous reflections on the history of the absorbingly interesting building they have in their care. I am also grateful to John Blair, Michael Hare, Simon Keynes, Veronica Ortenberg and (or course) Jenny Wormald for constructive criticisms and helpful suggestions as my thoughts took what shape they have.

2.   The 'Complete List of Churches' in H.M. (& A.J.) Taylor, *Anglo-Saxon Architecture* (3 vols, Cambridge, 1965, 1978), III, pp. 767-72, numbers 267, their 'Appendix F' (pp. 1071-7) adding twelve more; but seventeen are little more than archaeologically exposed foundations (pp. 738, 741-6, 751-5). For two expert modern views that would both prune and expand their *corpus* on general or specific grounds, see R. Gem, 'The English Parish Church in the 11th and Early 12th Centuries: a Great Rebuilding?', and T. Tatton-Brown, 'The Churches of Canterbury Diocese in the 11th Century', in J. Blair, ed., *Minsters and Parish Churches: the Local Church in Transition, 950-1200* (Oxford University Committee for Archaeology 17, 1988), pp. 21-30, 105-18. A review of the Taylors' work also noting the dissonance of historial and architectural records is S. Keynes (with M. & B.K. Biddle, R. Cramp, M. Gatch), '*Anglo-Saxon Architecture* and Anglo-Saxon Studies: a review', *Anglo Saxon England* 14 (1985), pp. 293-317, at pp. 293-302.

3.   The Taylors give references to Bede for Bradwell, Breedon (not in their 'Complete List'), St Martin's Canterbury, Hackness and Hart, as well as Bosham where the church is not of the Bedan period; to Durham sources for Billingham, Bywell, Corbridge, Seaham, Sockburn, Staindrop and ? Whittingham; to William of Malmesbury for Bradford, Gloucester and Wareham; to the *Anglo-Saxon Chronicle* for Reculver, Repton and Wimborne; to St Albans' *Gesta Abbatum* for two local churches; and to Felix's *Life of Guthlac*, Goscelin, John of Worcester, Hugh Candidus, *Liber Eliensis* and a York Chronicle for Repton, Much Wenlock, Repton again, Hadstock, Brixworth and Stow respectively. For narratives on Dover and Minster-Sheppey, see D. Rollason, *The Mildrith Legend: a Study in Early Medieval Hagiography in England* (Leicester, 1982).

4.   References are to P.H. Sawyer, ed., *Anglo-Saxon Charters: an Annotated list and Bibliography* (Royal Historical Society, 1968) [S]: Bakewell (not in the 'Complete List'), S 548; Bibury, S 1254; Breedon, S 72; Dover, S 22, 1400, 1439, 1461; Minster-Sheppey, S22; Much Wenlock, S 1254; Reculver, S 8, 22, 31, 38, 546, 1390, 1436: Stow, S 1478; West Mersea, S 1483, 1486, 1494: White Notley, S 1522. Tatton-Brown, p. 110, gives reasons for including St Mary's Dover in this and the above list, but not the well-documented Lyminge churches.

5.   S 1187. I have already discussed this case in detail in W. Davies and P. Fouracre,

eds, *The Settlement of Disputes in Early Medieval Europe* (Cambridge, 1986), pp. 152-7; and see also the Appendix above.

6. S 1433.

7. S 139/146, 58/59; see further Appendix above.

8. I have given a review of the high points of the controversy, and made a first attempt at a fresh approach to it, in *Bede and the Conversion of England: the Charter evidence* (Jarrow lecture, 1984), pp. 19-23. I shall be returning to the subject at greater length in chapter 11 of my *The Making of English Law: King Alfred to the Norman Conquest* (Oxford, 1995/6).

9. For a brilliant account of how the foundation of nunneries was promoted by the property strategies of an early Germanic aristocracy, see K.J. Leyser, *Rule and Conflict in an Early Medieval Society: Ottonian Saxony* (2nd edn, Oxford, 1989), pp. 49-73.

10. Bede, 'Epistola ad Ecgberhtum', ed. C. Plummer, *Baedae Opera Historica* (2 vols, Oxford, 1896) 12, pp. 415-6; tr. D. Whitelock, *English Historical Documents, Vol I* (2nd edn, London, 1979), pp. 805-6.

11. For one example, see Campbell, *Anglo-Saxons*, p. 123.

12. S 1442; Laws of Alfred 41, tr. Whitelock, *Eng. Hist. Docs,* p. 415.

13. E.g. S 1500, 1510.

14. *The Anglo-Saxon Chronicle*: 807, ed. & tr. D. Whitelock *et al.* (London, 1961), p. 39. This volume, compounded of the versions in *Eng. Hist. Docs*, Vols I & II, is the most convenient means of access to the *Chronicle*, and references are henceforth taken from it [ASC].

15. Michael Hare has kindly drawn my attention to evidence that there were early houses of both men and women at Berkeley, and suggests that 'tensions between the two communities' may explain the Berkeley claim.

16. Wulfred's campaign, indeed the whole issue of minster reform, has been illuminated as never before by Nicholas Brooks, *The Early History of the Church of Canterbury* (Leicester, 1984), pp. 175-206

17. Brooks, *Canterbury*, pp. 167-8.

18. S1434, 1436, 1439; Brooks, *Canterbury*, pp. 183-6.

19. Osbern's *Life* is available only in the edition of H. Wharton, *Anglia Sacra* (2 vols, London, 1691) II, pp. 122-48 (here at pp. 123-4).

20. But Dunstan's patronage of Ælfheah might explain why he was later claimed as a product of Glastonbury: Brooks, *Canterbury*, p. 279.

21. D. Knowles, *The Monastic Order in England* (Cambridge, 2nd edn, 1961), pp. 52, 721.

22.   M. Lapidge, 'Byhrtferth and the *Vita S. Ecgwini*', *Medieval Studies* XLI (1979), pp. 331-53, at pp. 339-40.

23.   Cf. A. Williams, '*Princeps Merciorum gentis*: the family, career and connections of Ælfhere, ealdorman of Mercia', *Anglo-Saxon England* 10 (1981), pp. 143-72, at p. 167.

24.   William of Malmesbury, *De Gestis Pontificum Anglorum*, ed. N.E.S.A. Hamilton (Rolls Series, 1870), p. 169; Florence of Worcester, *Chronicon*, ed. B. Thorpe (London,1848) I, p. 147. See M. Brett, 'John of Worcester and his Contemporaries', *The Writing of History in the Middle Ages: Essays presented to R.W. Southern*, ed. R.H.C. Davis & J.M. Wallace-Hadrill (Oxford, 1981), pp. 104-26.

25.   R.W. Southern, *Saint Anselm and his Biographer* (Cambridge, 1961), pp. 217, 249.

26.   See the conspectus of modern continental views in P. Wormald, 'Æthelwold and his continental counterparts: contact, comparison, contrast', *Bishop Æthelwold: His Career and Influence*, ed. B. Yorke (Woodbridge, 1988), pp. 13-42, at pp. 21, 28-9.

27.   *ASC* 1016, 1053 'D', 1056 'C' 'D', pp. 96, 128, 132-3; Florence, *Chron*. 1016, 1053,1056, I, pp. 178, 211, 215 (the latter two references are of course more likely to be to the '*regia aula* ', of which 'Odda's chapel' was part, than to St Mary's Church itself).

28.   The essential introduction to *Chronicle* studies and problems is Whitelock's (as above, n. 14), revised and updated in *Eng. Hist. Docs,* 2nd edn (as n. 10), pp. 113-21.

29.   I an grateful to Dr C.R. Hart for showing me a paper on 'The English Chronicles from 1018 to 1042', argung that 'D' used a lost set of Latin Worcester annals better represented by John's text; see his 'The Early Sections of the Worcester Chronicle',*Jnl. Med. Hist.* 9 (1983), pp. 251-315. Since our arguments come to much the same thing, it seemed best to leave mine more or less as they orginally stood.

30.   I. Atkins, 'The orgin of the later part of the Saxon Chronicle known as D',*Eng. Hist. Rev.* LV (1940), pp. 8-26.

31.   William of Malmesbury, *Vita Wulfstani*, ed. R.R. Darlington (Camden Society 3rd series XL, 1928) pp. 56-7, with p. xxxviii, n. 2. I owe this point to Dr Ortenberg.

32.   C. Plummer, ed., *Two of the Saxon Chronicles Parallel (*2 vols, Oxford, 1892-9) II, pp.lxxv-lxxvii.

33.   Whitelock (as n. 28); see also D. Whitelock, ed., *The Peterborough Chronicle* (Early English Manuscripts in Facsimile IV, Copenhagen 1954), pp. 28-9.

34.   *ASC* 946, 1048, 1053, pp. 72, 111, 127. Cf. (e.g.) 940, 1033, 1044, 1049, 1052, 1063, pp. 70, 102, 108, 114, 122, 136 (and below, n. 36).

35.   M. Lapidge, 'Byrhtferth of Ramsey and the early sections of the *Historia Regum* attributed to Symeon of Durham', *Anglo-Saxon England* 10 (1982), pp. 97-122;

simultaneously with C.R. Hart, 'Byrhtferth's Northumbrian Chronicle', *Eng. Hist. Rev.* XCVII (1982), pp. 558-82.

36. *ASC* 1046, 1053, 1054, 1058, 1061, pp. 109, 128-9, 134-5; cf. 1049, p.114 (Ealdred let down by lack of support in his efforts to repel Irish raiders). For an arresting suggestion about Ealdred's consecration of Gloucester, see Michael Hare's 1992 Deerhurst lecture, *The two Anglo-Saxon minsters of Gloucester* (1993), pp.

37. *ASC* 1051, p. 120.

38. *ASC* 1066, p. 145; 'Chronica Pontificum Ecclesiae Eboracensis', ed. J. Raine, *Historians of the Church of York and its Archbishops* (3 vols, Rolls Series, 1879-86) II, pp. 350-3.

39. ASC 1054, 1057, 1066, pp. 129, 133, 143. For one important outcome of Ealdred's Cologne visit, see M. Lapidge, 'The Origin of CCCC 163', *Transactions of the Cambridge Bibliographical Society* VIII (1982), pp. 18-28; and J.L. Nelson, 'The Rites of the Conqueror', *Proceedings of the Fourth Battle Conference on Anglo-Norman Studies*, ed. R.A. Brown (Woodbridge, 1982), pp. 117-32, repr. in her *Politics and Ritual in Early Medieval Europe* (London, 1986), pp. 389-99.

40. R.C. van Caenegem, ed. & tr., *English Lawsuits from William I to Richard I* (2 vols, Selden Society 106-7, 1990-1) I, pp. 3-6. cf. M. Richter, *Canterbury Professions* (Canterbury & York Society LXVII, 1972), p. 26.

41. See Knowles, *Monastic Order* (as n. 21), pp. 166-70; it may not be irrelevant that Turgot, almost certainly the biographer of St Margaret, was an early associate of Aldwin, the West Midlander who led the northern revival.

42. Though I have tried to avoid the more Gordian of *Chronicle* knots in my text, evaded issues make for long footnotes, and it is necessary to take some account of the most strongly argued of the alternatives to an 'Ealdred' provenance for the 'D' text, namely Canterbury. The arguments in its favour are of two types. Firstly, there are entries of apparently Canterbury interest 1019-23 (Hart, forthcoming as n. 29, and Dr M. K. Lawson's important new book, *Cnut* (London, 1993), pp. 52-5); since the hand that wrote 'D's' annals 1016-51 was apparently the same as that of its concluding section 1071-9 (N.R. Ker, *Catalogue of Manuscripts Containing Anglo-Saxon*, Oxford, 1957, p. 254), a possible implication is that the text was finished at Canterbury. Arguments of this type are, however, open to objections on the point of principle put earlier in my text: only when microcosmic details merge to form a macrocosmic pattern, as they do in Ealdred's case, do they begin to argue for the provenance of a whole text rather than that of one of its many possible sources. Most of the 1019-23 entries relate somehow or other to the archbishopric; that the new archbishop was consecrated by Wulfstan and accompanied on his journey to receive the pallium by Abbot Leofwine of Ely are merely two of numerous ways in which news of the metropolitan see might achieve wider circulation (see also n. 43). The second approach argues from relationships between extant texts, and has recently been expounded with characteristically awesome learning by Dr David Dumville, 'Some Aspects of Annalistic Writing at

Canterbury in the Eleventh and Early Twelfth Centuries', *Peritia* 2 (1983), pp. 23-57, especially at pp. 31-8, 53. The argument here (to summarize and over-simplify) is that the 'E' version of the Chronicle depends on a Canterbury (and probably St. Augustine's) source until at least the early 1060s, and that 'D' and 'E' are close in their (largely northern) orientation 1065-76. But it remains unclear why it is *necessary* to believe as he does that 'D' must have drawn on 'E's' source. 'D' in its present form is, as has been said, a conflation, and one to which 'C' or its *doppelgänger* has made a significant contribution. But there is no such relationship between 'D' and 'E' for the forty years before 1065, in which period 'D' has much of its own to offer (nn. 34, 36-7, 39 above); a vignette of their differences is at 1049, p. 115, where 'D' denies knowledge of 'what bishops ... and in particular what abbots' attended the Council of Rheims, but identifies the abbeys of two as St Augustine's and Ramsey; while 'E' names a bishop and two abbots but only one abbey! Further, 'E' is itself a conflation, and one with no distinctively Canterbury elements after 1063. So there seems to be no reason in principle why the conflationary mix available to its Peterborough compiler in 1121 should not have included *both* a Canterbury text (with 'northern recension' features down to 975 already built in) *and* later-eleventh-century northern annals close to, but not identical with, those of 'D'. In other words, 'E' could just as well be considered indebted to northern annals shared by 'D', as 'D' to have exploited northern material made available at Canterbury by 'E's' source.

43. *ASC* 1023, pp. 99-100. On the other hand, Archbishop Wulfstan's property deals had made his memory less than evergreen at Worcester: D. Whitelock, ed., *Sermo Lupi ad Anglos* (London, 3rd edn, 1963), pp. 8-9.

44. See *Anglo-Saxon Charters*, ed. & tr. A.J. Robertson (Cambridge, 2nd edn, 1956), pp. 456-8.

45. *Domesday Book*, ed. A. Farley (London, 1783), f. 166b (*Domesday Book, Gloucestershire*, ed. & tr. J.S. Moore, (Chichester, 1982) 19:1-2, 20); cf. Knowles, *Monastic Order* (as n. 21), pp. 702-3.

46. S 1143, 1146; S 1551; S 1043, 1046. *Regesta Regum Anglo-Normannorum*, vol. I, ed. H.W.C. Davis (Oxford, 1912) no. 32.

47. See the brilliant edition and translation of E. Panofsky, *Abbot Suger on the Abbey-Church of St-Denis* (Princeton, 2nd edn, 1979).

48. *Gesta Pontificum* (as n. 24). Dr Blair helpfully points out to me that Wing and Wootton Wawen are also churches with significant pre-conquest fabric which had alien lords after 1066; while Brixworth, and even Jarrow and Monkwearmouth, were dependencies of cathedrals. It can be added that the wealth of St Mary's Stow (above, p. 2 and n. 4) was eventually much reduced in favour of the new post-conquest bishopric at Lincoln: Taylor & Taylor, *Anglo-Saxon Architecture* II, p. 585.